BEND Y

LOUISE!

A Pickleball Primer

Jackie Freeman & Karen Worthy

Illustrated by Kevin Fales

"Jack and Louise,
grandchildren of mine,
let's learn something new.
Let's say it in rhyme."

"Pickleball! Pickleball!
It's my favorite sport.
Now grab your gym shoes,
and we'll head to the court."
Pickleball Fun Facts
Pickleball is the fastest-growing adult sport in the United States.

"This sport is not something
to drink or to eat.
Pickles in a jar?
No, not that kind of treat."

"Oh, please," says Louise.
"We like to sit.
Our games don't require
a club or a mitt."

"No, no, you two.
Get off that couch!
Don't be so lazy!
And don't be a grouch!"
Pickleball Fun Facts
Children spend an average of 4-6 hours daily on screen time.

"Now let me show you
how fun it can be,
for folks young and old.
Come on, you'll see!"

"Pile into the car.
Off we go to the court,
where I'll teach you about
this Pickleball sport."

"Drink plenty of water
and stretch head to toe,
to keep your body healthy.
That's important, you know."

"These Pickleball paddles
are shaped like your head.
They come in bright colors:
white, blue, pink, and red."

Pickleball Fun Facts

A pickleball paddle is smaller than a tennis racquet, but larger than a ping pong paddle and made of lightweight composite materials.

Pickleball Fun Facts

Pickleballs are made of durable plastic with several holes. They look like a whiffle ball.

"The holes in the balls
make them light as can be
and easy to hit,
as you will soon see."

Jack asks a question
as he points to a court.
"How many people
can play this sport?"

"I see four over there
and two over here.
This is confusing!
Please, make it clear."

"We can play **one-on-one**,
or on teams of two.
Today you and Louise
will play Martin and Sue."

"This looks like **tennis**,"
Louise quickly observes.
"Are the rules very different?
Do they have the same serves?"

"This paddle is smaller, but the courts look the same. Let's review a few rules before starting the game."

Pickleball Fun Facts

In the Non-Volley Zone, a player is not allowed to strike the ball unless it bounces first.

"Run up near the **kitchen**.
It's a great place to play.
But first let the ball bounce,
then hit it away."

"A kitchen here
on the Pickleball court?
You cook while you play?
What a strange kind of sport!"

"I think we are ready!
Sue will begin.
First side to score eleven
is the team that will win."

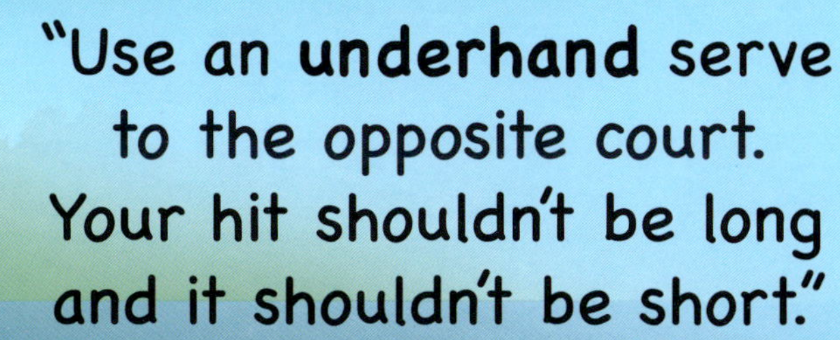

"Use an **underhand** serve
to the opposite court.
Your hit shouldn't be long
and it shouldn't be short."

"When it's your turn to serve,
Martin, Sue, Jack, and Louise,
announce your score,
then state theirs, please."

"They'll send the ball
over the net to your side.
Hit hard or hit soft?
You'll soon learn to decide."

"Direct the ball back.
Don't aim it too wide.
You only score
on the serving side."

"Learning will take time,
but just wait and see.
You'll soon understand
that patience is key."

"There are so many rules to think about. Grandma, what happens if I strike out?"

"No strikes or passes are found in this game. Having barrels of fun is our first aim!"

"Your paddle skills
will improve very fast.
Mastering the rules
is an easy task."
HMMM HMMM
Pickleball Rules
Pickleball Fun Facts
Running backwards is the number one cause of falls on the pickleball court.
"Practice and practice.
You'll win matches soon.
Pickleball's as easy
as humming a tune."

"BEND YOUR KNEES, LOUISE!"
Grandma points and calls out,
"Use your legs and your knees!
That's what I'm talking about!"

"Practice and practice
and learn how to **drill**.
You'll soon learn to score,
using every new skill."

"We have **dinking** and **lobs**,
and the **third shot drop**.
You'll soon get so good
you won't want to stop!"

Back and forth,
the Pickleball soars.
When the game is over,
Louise calls the score.

"We got eleven!
Martin and Sue got four.
We're catching on fast!
Can we play some more?"

Jack pumps his fist.
"Grandma, we WON!"
Now the kids both agree.
"THIS PICKLEBALL GAME
IS TOTALLY FUN!"

GLOSSARY

Cross-Court: The court diagonally opposite your court.

Dinking: Soft shots that are intended to arc over the net and land within the non-volley zone.

Drill: A physical or mental exercise aimed at perfecting a skill, especially with regular practice.

Kitchen: The area seven feet from the net on each side, also known as the non-volley zone.

Lobs: A lofted shot that sends the ball high overhead and deep into the other court.

One-on-one: Playing directly against a single opposing player.

Tennis: A game played on a rectangular court by two players or two pairs of players equipped with racquets, in which a ball is driven back and forth over a low net that divides the court in half.

Third Shot Drop: A shot performed at or near the baseline that lands softly in the opponent's kitchen. The shot is designed with mostly one thing in mind: to get your team to the net.

Underhand Serve: A serve is made with an underhand stroke. The paddle head must be below the server's wrist when it hits the ball.

Authors: Jackie Freeman & Karen Worthy
Illustrated by Kevin Fales

Published by Miriam Laundry Publishing Corporation
www.MiriamLaundry.com

ISBN 978-0-9938964-9-1
e-Book ISBN 978-1-990107-02-3

Library of Congress Control Number: 2020920513

Printed in USA
at Graphics East, Roseville, Michigan

10 9 8 7 6 5 4 3 2 1